Salads on the Run: The Top 50 Mason Jar Salad Recipes That Are Quick, Crafty, and Great on the Go

D1166151

Disclaimer and Terms of Use: Effort has been made to ensure that the information in this book is accurate and complete, however, the author and the publisher do not warrant the accuracy of the information, text and graphics contained within the book due to the rapidly changing nature of science, research, known and unknown facts and internet. The Author and the publisher do not hold any responsibility for errors, omissions or contrary interpretation of the subject matter herein. This book is presented solely for motivational and informational purposes only.

Table of Contents

Mojito fruit salad 97

Vegetable and Meat Based salads

Spinach salad with strawberry vinaigrette

Serves: 1

Time: 10 minutes + inactive time

Ingredients:

- ¼ cup cooked quinoa
- 4 strawberries, hulled and sliced
- 1 ½ cups baby spinach, fresh
- ¼ cup crumbled feta
- 1 tablespoon sliced onions
- ½ tablespoon sunflower seeds
- 2 tablespoons extra-virgin olive oil
- 1 tablespoon fresh lime juice
- 1 teaspoon Dijon mustard
- 2 teaspoons strawberry preserves
- 1 tablespoon white wine vinegar
- Salt and pepper – to taste

Directions:

1. Whisk together olive oil, lime juice, strawberry preserves, mustard and vinegar; season to taste.
2. Pour into standard Mason jar and top with cooked quinoa. Add strawberry slices, sunflower seeds and crumbled feta.
3. Finally place in the baby spinach and chill for 15 minutes before serving. Shale before use.

Mexican salad in jar

Serves: 1

Time: 10 minutes

Ingredients:

- ¼ cup cooked brown rice
- ¼ cup cooked chickpeas
- 2 tablespoons salsa
- 2 grape tomatoes, halved
- 1 tablespoon fresh cilantro, chopped
- ½ small onion, sliced thinly
- 1 cup romaine lettuce, chopped
- 2 tablespoons extra-virgin olive oil
- 1 teaspoon cumin, ground
- 2 tablespoons lime juice
- Pinch of red pepper flakes
- Salt and pepper – to taste

Directions:

1. Whisk together olive oil, cumin, lime juice, pepper flakes and season to taste; transfer into standard Mason jar.
2. Add rice and chickpeas. Top with salsa, onions, cilantro, halved tomatoes and lettuce.
3. Stir or shake before use, so vinaigrette coats all ingredients.

Nutrition Facts

Serving Size 499 g

Amount Per Serving

Calories 677	Calories from Fat 301

	% Daily Value*
Total Fat 33.5g	52%
Saturated Fat 4.7g	23%
Cholesterol 0mg	0%
Sodium 226mg	9%
Potassium 1419mg	41%
Total Carbohydrates 84.1g	28%
Dietary Fiber 15.2g	61%
Sugars 14.9g	
Protein 16.9g	

Vitamin A 47%	•	Vitamin C 70%
Calcium 13%	•	Iron 43%

Nutrition Grade A

* Based on a 2000 calorie diet

Asian Tofu salad with sesame dressing

Serves: 1

Time: 12 minutes + inactive time

Ingredients:

- 1.5oz. pressed and cubed extra-firm tofu
- 1 cucumber, chopped
- 1 tablespoon sunflower seeds
- 2 tablespoons sprouted lentils
- 1 tablespoon fresh parsley, chopped
- ½ red bell pepper sliced into thin strips
- 1 cup chopped romaine lettuce
- 1 tablespoon tahini – sesame paste
- 1 teaspoon honey
- ¼ teaspoon salt, oregano and black pepper
- 1 teaspoon sesame oil
- 1 tablespoon lemon juice
- 1 tablespoon white wine vinegar
- 1 clove garlic, minced
- Pinch of red pepper flakes

Directions:

1. Place together tahini, honey, spices, oregano, garlic, red pepper flakes, sesame oil, lemon juice and vinegar into standard Mason jar. Apply the lid and shake until emulsified.
2. Add tofu, red bell pepper, sprouts, sunflower seeds, parsley, cucumbers and romaine lettuce.
3. Refrigerate for 15 minutes and shake before use.

Nutrition Facts

Serving Size 465 g

Amount Per Serving

Calories 274   Calories from Fat 165

% Daily Value*

Total Fat 18.3g	**28%**
Saturated Fat 2.5g	**13%**
Trans Fat 0.0g	
Cholesterol 0mg	**0%**
Sodium 614mg	**26%**
Potassium 593mg	**17%**
Total Carbohydrates 22.6g	**8%**
Dietary Fiber 4.5g	**18%**
Sugars 11.8g	
Protein 10.1g	

Vitamin A 13% •	Vitamin C 38%
Calcium 7% •	Iron 37%

Nutrition Grade B

* Based on a 2000 calorie diet

Spinach salad with orange vinaigrette

Serves: 1

Time: 10 minutes

Ingredients:

- ¼ cup cooked quinoa
- 1 clementine, cut into wedges
- 1 tablespoon pine nuts
- ½ onion, small, thinly sliced
- 1 tablespoon sprouted lentils
- 1 cup baby spinach
- ½ cup romaine lettuce
- 2 tablespoons orange marmalade
- Salt and pepper- to taste
- 1 pinch red pepper flakes
- 2 teaspoons extra-virgin olive oil
- 2 tablespoons apple cider vinegar

Directions:

1. Whisk together in a small bowl the orange marmalade, red pepper flakes, olive oil, apple cider vinegar and season to taste.
2. Pour into standard Mason jar; add cooked quinoa, clementine wedges, onion, sprouts, pine nuts, lettuce and spinach.
3. Apply the lid and shake before use.

Nutrition Facts

Serving Size 249 g

Amount Per Serving

Calories 438   Calories from Fat 163

	% Daily Value*
Total Fat 18.1g	28%
Saturated Fat 2.1g	10%
Trans Fat 0.0g	
Cholesterol 0mg	0%
Sodium 54mg	2%
Potassium 634mg	18%
Total Carbohydrates 63.4g	21%
Dietary Fiber 5.6g	23%
Sugars 27.2g	
Protein 9.4g	

Vitamin A 59%	•	Vitamin C 27%
Calcium 8%	•	Iron 24%

Nutrition Grade B+

* Based on a 2000 calorie diet

Taco jar salad

Serves: 1

Time: 20 minutes

Ingredients:

- 3oz. ground turkey
- 1oz. Black beans, can, rinsed and drained
- 2 tablespoons water
- 1 mini cucumber, sliced
- ¼ avocado, chopped
- 1 tablespoon onion, sliced
- 2 tablespoons salsa
- 1 tablespoon Greek yogurt
- 1 cup Romaine lettuce, chopped
- 3 cherry tomatoes, halved
- 1 teaspoon Taco seasoning
- 1 tablespoon lime juice
- 1oz. pickled jalapenos, drained and chopped

Directions:

1. In a medium pan cook ground turkey until no longer pink.
2. Add black beans and season with taco seasoning. Add water and stir all. Let the mixture cool.
3. Place salsa in bottom of the jar; add yogurt, tomatoes, cucumbers, onion, jalapenos, avocado, taco meat and lettuce. Apply the lid and shake before use.

Nutrition Facts

Serving Size 379 g

Amount Per Serving

Calories 398	Calories from Fat 175

	% Daily Value*
Total Fat 19.4g	30%
Saturated Fat 3.7g	18%
Trans Fat 0.0g	
Cholesterol 82mg	27%
Sodium 291mg	12%
Potassium 1359mg	39%
Total Carbohydrates 31.4g	10%
Dietary Fiber 10.2g	41%
Sugars 6.0g	
Protein 30.9g	

Vitamin A 24%	•	Vitamin C 43%
Calcium 9%	•	Iron 29%

Nutrition Grade A

* Based on a 2000 calorie diet

Caesar salad in jar

Serves: 1

Time: 10 minutes

Ingredients:

-   2 cups kale, stems removed, torn into bite-size pieces
-   1 cup cucumber, diced
-   ½ avocado, diced
-   ¼ cup cherry tomatoes, halved

- 1 tablespoon parmesan, shredded
- 2.5oz. chicken, grilled and cut into chunks
- 1 lemon, juiced and zest
- 1 egg
- 1 cup extra-virgin olive oil
- 6 anchovies, fillets
- 2 garlic cloves, minced
- 1 egg yolk
- Salt and pepper – to taste
- Some bread croutons

Directions:

1. Grate the zest from lemon. Place the zest, garlic and anchovies in a food blender; process until you get a nice paste.
2. Add egg yolk, pinch of salt and squeeze of lemon juice; pulse to combine.
3. While blender is running pour in olive oil, drop at the time, until mixture is emulsified.
4. Pour the mixture, 2 tablespoons in a standard Mason jar; top with kale, cucumber, cherry tomatoes, avocado, chicken, parmesan and croutons. Shake before use.

Nutrition Facts

Serving Size 408 g

Amount Per Serving

Calories 925	Calories from Fat 629

% Daily Value*

Total Fat 69.9g	108%
Saturated Fat 14.2g	71%
Trans Fat 0.0g	
Cholesterol 519mg	173%
Sodium 4529mg	189%
Potassium 1512mg	43%
Total Carbohydrates 15.1g	5%
Dietary Fiber 7.4g	29%
Sugars 1.0g	
Protein 62.6g	

Vitamin A 116%	•	Vitamin C 87%
Calcium 40%	•	Iron 48%

Nutrition Grade B

* Based on a 2000 calorie diet

Caprese salad in jar

Serves: 2

Time: 10 minutes

Ingredients:

- 5oz. mozzarella balls
- ½ cup baby spinach
- 1 cup cooked orzo pasta
- 4 tablespoons balsamic vinegar
- 1 cup cherry tomatoes, like red, yellow, orange

Directions:

1. Divide the balsamic vinegar between two standard Mason jars.
2. Divide the mozzarellas balls and top with ingredients in following order; tomatoes, spinach and orzo pasta, dividing all evenly.
3. You can refrigerate or serve immediately, just make sure to shake well before use.

Nutrition Facts

Serving Size 262 g

Amount Per Serving

Calories 436	Calories from Fat 152
	% Daily Value*
Total Fat 16.8g	26%
Saturated Fat 7.8g	39%
Trans Fat 0.0g	
Cholesterol 72mg	24%
Sodium 231mg	10%
Potassium 392mg	11%
Total Carbohydrates 39.1g	13%
Dietary Fiber 1.2g	5%
Sugars 2.5g	
Protein 20.9g	

Vitamin A 30%	•	Vitamin C 24%
Calcium 46%	•	Iron 15%

Nutrition Grade B-

* Based on a 2000 calorie diet

Mediterranean salad in jar

Serves: 2

Time: 10 minutes

Ingredients:

- 1 cup fire-roasted bell peppers
- 1 cup feta cheese, crumbled
- 1 cup pitted olives, like Kalamata
- 1 cup cucumber, chopped
- 4 tablespoons red wine vinaigrette
- 1 cup red sugar plum tomatoes
- 1 cup red onion, chopped

Directions:

1. Divide the vinaigrette between two standard Mason jars.
2. Top with ingredients, following this order; tomatoes, cucumbers, olives, peppers, onion and crumbled feta, all dividing evenly between the jars.
3. Apply the lid and shake well before serving.

Nutrition Facts

Serving Size 447 g

Amount Per Serving

Calories 429	Calories from Fat 254

	% Daily Value*
Total Fat 28.3g	43%
Saturated Fat 12.7g	63%
Trans Fat 0.0g	
Cholesterol 67mg	22%
Sodium 2243mg	93%
Potassium 212mg	6%
Total Carbohydrates 25.8g	9%
Dietary Fiber 3.6g	15%
Sugars 15.6g	
Protein 12.2g	

Vitamin A 146%	•	Vitamin C 170%
Calcium 45%	•	Iron 17%

Nutrition Grade B-

* Based on a 2000 calorie diet

Eggs-bacon salad in jar

Serves: 4

Time: 12 minutes

Ingredients:

- 2 cups lettuce, chopped like iceberg
- 2 cups chopped plum tomatoes
- 8 tablespoons red wine vinaigrette
- 4 tablespoons blue cheese, crumbled
- 2 cups chicken, grilled and chopped
- 4 hardboiled eggs, sliced
- 2 cups avocado
- 2 tablespoons lemon juice
- 2 cups bacon, crumbled
- 4 tablespoons scallions, chopped

Directions:

1. Toss the avocado with lemon juice in a bowl.
2. Divide the vinaigrette between four Mason jars.
3. Top with chicken, tomatoes, eggs, bacon, avocado, scallions, blue cheese and salad, all dividing evenly between the jars.
4. Shake well before use.

Nutrition Facts

Serving Size 357 g

Amount Per Serving

Calories 426   Calories from Fat 256

% Daily Value*

Total Fat 28.5g	44%
Saturated Fat 7.6g	38%
Trans Fat 0.0g	
Cholesterol 224mg	75%
Sodium 404mg	17%
Potassium 814mg	23%
Total Carbohydrates 13.8g	5%
Dietary Fiber 6.2g	25%
Sugars 5.9g	
Protein 30.4g	

Vitamin A 21%	•	Vitamin C 57%
Calcium 10%	•	Iron 18%

Nutrition Grade B

* Based on a 2000 calorie diet

Fresh and colorful salad with apples

Serves: 1

Time: 15 minutes

Ingredients:

- 2 radishes, thinly sliced
- 1 celery stalk, diced
- ¼ green apple, sliced
- 3 tablespoons raw almond butter
- 1 tablespoon maple syrup
- 1 tablespoon rice wine vinegar
- 3 cups mixed greens
- 2 teaspoons sesame oil
- ¼ cup walnuts, crushed
- Salt – to taste

Directions:

1. Combine rice wine vinegar, sesame oil and almond butter in a bowl; whisk until blended and transfer two tablespoons into standard Mason jar.
2. Top with radishes, apples, celery, walnuts and mixed greens.
3. Apply the lid, shake well and serve.

Nutrition Facts

Serving Size 740 g

Amount Per Serving

Calories 1,023	Calories from Fat 500

	% Daily Value*
Total Fat 55.6g	86%
Saturated Fat 5.1g	25%
Trans Fat 0.0g	
Cholesterol 0mg	0%
Sodium 211mg	9%
Potassium 1605mg	46%
Total Carbohydrates 103.5g	35%
Dietary Fiber 29.4g	118%
Sugars 34.4g	
Protein 33.6g	

Vitamin A 469%	•	Vitamin C 39%
Calcium 31%	•	Iron 43%

Nutrition Grade A

* Based on a 2000 calorie diet

Artichoke salad

Serves: 1

Time: 10 minutes

Ingredients:

- 1 tablespoon tamari sauce
- 1 tablespoon juice from marinated artichoke hears
- 3 marinated artichoke hearts, quartered
- 2 white mushrooms, sliced
- 2 tablespoons red bell pepper, chopped
- ¼ cup broccoli florets
- ¼ cup chickpeas, cooked
- 1 cup kale, stems removed, torn into bite size pieces
- Salt and pepper – to taste

Directions:

1. Place the tamari sauce, artichoke liquid and seasonings in a standard mason jar; apply the lid and shake until combined.
2. Place kale in a bowl and sprinkle with salt; squeeze kale until starts to wilt.
3. Begin layering salad; top the dressing with artichokes, mushrooms, red bell peppers, broccoli, chickpeas and kale.
4. Serve immediately.

Nutrition Facts

Serving Size 294 g

Amount Per Serving

Calories 246	Calories from Fat 29

% Daily Value*

Total Fat 3.3g	5%
Trans Fat 0.0g	
Cholesterol 0mg	0%
Sodium 991mg	41%
Potassium 992mg	28%
Total Carbohydrates 43.1g	14%
Dietary Fiber 11.0g	44%
Sugars 8.1g	
Protein 15.6g	

Vitamin A 221%	•	Vitamin C 212%
Calcium 15%	•	Iron 30%

Nutrition Grade A

* Based on a 2000 calorie diet

Asian cabbage salad

Serves: 1

Time: 10 minutes

Ingredients:

- 1 tablespoon soy sauce
- 1 teaspoon lime juice
- 1 teaspoon almond butter
- ¼ teaspoon hot sauce
- ½ teaspoon maple syrup
- 2 teaspoons chickpea miso
- ½ cup purple cabbage, shredded
- 1 tablespoon spring onions, chopped
- ¼ cup sliced radish
- 1 teaspoon sesame seeds, toasted
- ¼ cup sugar snap peas, stings removed and sliced
- 2 tablespoons fresh cilantro, chopped

Directions:

1. Combine soy sauce, lime juice, hot sauce, almond butter, maple syrup and chickpea miso in standard Mason jar. Apply the jar lid and shake well until blended.
2. Begin layering salad in the next order; add cabbage, followed with spring onions, radish, sesame seeds, snap peas and cilantro.
3. Chill or serve immediately.

Nutrition Facts

Serving Size 127 g

Amount Per Serving

Calories 111	Calories from Fat 42

% Daily Value*

Total Fat 4.6g	7%
Saturated Fat 0.5g	3%
Trans Fat 0.0g	
Cholesterol 0mg	0%
Sodium 1294mg	54%
Potassium 283mg	8%
Total Carbohydrates 13.8g	5%
Dietary Fiber 2.6g	11%
Sugars 4.7g	
Protein 4.4g	

Vitamin A 8%	•	Vitamin C 49%
Calcium 8%	•	Iron 10%

Nutrition Grade A

* Based on a 2000 calorie diet

Bean salad with creamy dressing

Serves: 1

Time: 15 minutes

Ingredients:

- 3 tablespoons cashews, soaked in water for 1 hour
- ¼ teaspoon chipotle powder
- 1 teaspoon nutritional yeast
- 1 garlic clove, crushed
- 2 teaspoons lime juice
- ¼ teaspoon salt
- ¼ cup can black beans, drained and rinsed
- 2 tablespoons sliced red onion
- 1 tablespoon green bell pepper, chopped
- 3 cherry tomatoes, halved
- ½ cup arugula
- 2 tablespoons fresh cilantro, chopped
- ¼ avocado, diced

- 1 tablespoon pumpkin seeds, toasted

Directions:

1. Rinse cashews and place in standard Mason jar; add chipotle powder, lime juice, nutritional yeast, garlic and salt. Apply the blender base on the jar and process the ingredients until smooth and creamy.
2. Top the dressing with following ingredients; black beans, red onion, tomatoes, bell pepper, arugula, cilantro, avocado and pumpkin seeds.
3. Stir well or shake before use.

Nutrition Facts

Serving Size 200 g

Amount Per Serving

Calories 389	Calories from Fat 238

	% Daily Value*
Total Fat 26.4g	41%
Saturated Fat 5.2g	26%
Trans Fat 0.0g	
Cholesterol 0mg	0%
Sodium 844mg	35%
Potassium 900mg	26%
Total Carbohydrates 31.5g	11%
Dietary Fiber 9.4g	38%
Sugars 3.7g	
Protein 12.9g	

Vitamin A 19%	•	Vitamin C 36%
Calcium 8%	•	Iron 31%

Nutrition Grade A-

* Based on a 2000 calorie diet

Arugula salad with beet

Serves: 1

Time: 10 minutes

Ingredients:

- 1 tablespoon red wine vinegar
- 1 garlic clove, minced
- 1 tablespoon extra-virgin olive oil
- 1 teaspoon honey
- 1 teaspoon fresh lime juice
- ¼ cup red beets, cooked and diced
- ¼ cup golden beets, diced
- ¼ cup Chioggia beets, diced
- ½ cup arugula
- ¼ green apple, cored and diced
- Salt and pepper – to taste

Directions:

1. Toss the apples with lime juice in a bowl.
2. Combine vinegar, garlic, olive oil, honey, pinch of salt and pepper in a standard Mason jar.
3. Apply the jar lid and shake to combine. Top the dressing with red beets, golden beets, Chioggia beets, arugula and apples.
4. Serve immediately or chilled.

Nutrition Facts

Serving Size 215 g

Amount Per Serving

Calories 227	Calories from Fat 129

	% Daily Value*
Total Fat 14.3g	22%
Saturated Fat 2.0g	10%
Trans Fat 0.0g	
Cholesterol 0mg	0%
Sodium 97mg	4%
Potassium 482mg	14%
Total Carbohydrates 25.3g	8%
Dietary Fiber 3.9g	16%
Sugars 20.0g	
Protein 2.6g	

Vitamin A 7%	•	Vitamin C 16%
Calcium 6%	•	Iron 8%

Nutrition Grade B

* Based on a 2000 calorie diet

Quinoa-potato salad

Serves: 1

Time: 10 minutes

Ingredients:

- 1 teaspoon extra-virgin olive oil
- 1 teaspoon lime juice
- 2 tablespoons balsamic vinegar
- ¼ cup cooked quinoa
- 2 tablespoons red onion, sliced
- ¼ cup sweet potato, cooked and diced
- 1 cup kale (massaged with sea salt to get ½ cup)
- 3 tablespoons pecan nuts, toasted
- Salt and pepper – to taste

Directions:

1. Place the olive oil, lime juice and balsamic vinegar in a standard Mason jar; season to taste and apply the jar lid; shake until blended.
2. Top the dressing with quinoa, red onion, potato, wilted kale and pecan nuts.
3. Serve immediately.

Nutrition Facts

Serving Size 257 g

Amount Per Serving

Calories 581   Calories from Fat 336

	% Daily Value*
Total Fat 37.4g	57%
Saturated Fat 4.0g	20%
Trans Fat 0.0g	
Cholesterol 0mg	0%
Sodium 52mg	2%
Potassium 1031mg	29%
Total Carbohydrates 52.8g	18%
Dietary Fiber 10.6g	42%
Sugars 5.7g	
Protein 13.7g	

Vitamin A 210%	•	Vitamin C 164%
Calcium 15%	•	Iron 33%

Nutrition Grade A-

* Based on a 2000 calorie diet

Mango and black bean salad

Serves: 1

Time: 10 minutes

Ingredients:

- 1 teaspoon lime juice
- 1 teaspoon cider vinegar
- ½ jalapeno, seeded and minced
- ¼ teaspoon honey
- 1 tablespoon extra-virgin olive oil
- ¼ cup quinoa, cooked
- ¼ avocado, diced
- ¼ mango, diced
- ¼ cup can black beans, drained and rinsed
- 1 tablespoon fresh cilantro, chopped
- 1 cup spinach
- Salt and pepper – to taste

Directions:

1. Toss the avocado with jalapeno and lime juice in a bowl.
2. Combine the cider vinegar, honey, salt, pepper and olive oil in a jar; apply the jar lid and shake well.
3. Begin layering salad over dressing in the next order; quinoa, avocado with jalapenos, mango, black beans, cilantro and spinach.
4. Serve immediately.

Nutrition Facts

Serving Size 251 g

Amount Per Serving

Calories 481   Calories from Fat 242

	% Daily Value*
Total Fat 26.9g	41%
Saturated Fat 4.4g	22%
Trans Fat 0.0g	
Cholesterol 0mg	0%
Sodium 271mg	11%
Potassium 963mg	28%
Total Carbohydrates 52.5g	18%
Dietary Fiber 10.8g	43%
Sugars 8.3g	
Protein 11.5g	

Vitamin A 65%	•	Vitamin C 41%
Calcium 9%	•	Iron 25%

Nutrition Grade B+

* Based on a 2000 calorie diet

Nicoise salad

Serves: 1

Time: 10 minutes

Ingredients:

- 1 red bell pepper, roasted and sliced
- 2oz. can tuna
- ½ cup sugar snap green beans, sliced and blanched
- ¼ cup can cannellini beans, rinsed and drained
- 4 fresh basil leaves
- ¼ cup Nicoise olives
- 1 tablespoon extra-virgin olive oil
- Salt and pepper – to taste

Directions:

1. Place the sliced bell peppers in a standard Mason jar.
2. Top with can tuna, green beans, cannellini beans, basil leaves and olives.
3. Drizzle with olive oil and season with salt. Apply he lid and shake gently.
4. Serve after.

Nutrition Facts

Serving Size 314 g

Amount Per Serving

Calories 289   Calories from Fat 162

% Daily Value*

Total Fat 18.0g	28%
Saturated Fat 2.5g	13%
Trans Fat 0.0g	
Cholesterol 20mg	7%
Sodium 467mg	19%
Potassium 375mg	11%
Total Carbohydrates 17.8g	6%
Dietary Fiber 6.5g	26%
Sugars 5.8g	
Protein 15.4g	

Vitamin A 87%	•	Vitamin C 269%
Calcium 7%	•	Iron 17%

Nutrition Grade B

* Based on a 2000 calorie diet

Wheat berry salad

Serves: 1

Time: 10 minutes

Ingredients:

- 2 tablespoons fresh orange juice
- 1 tablespoon apple juice
- 1 teaspoon cider vinegar
- 1 teaspoon ginger, minced
- 2 teaspoons lime juice
- ¼ cup cooked wheat berries
- ¼ cup quinoa, cooked
- ¼ cup edamame beans, chopped
- 2 tablespoon red bell pepper, diced
- 2 tablespoons green bell pepper, diced
- 2 tablespoon fresh parsley, copped
- Salt and pepper – to taste

Directions:

1. Place orange juice, apply juice, cider vinegar, lime juice, ginger, salt and pepper in a standard Mason jar; apply the jar lid and shake well.
2. Top with wheat berries, quinoa, edamame beans, red pepper, green pepper and parsley.
3. Shake well before serving.

Nutrition Facts

Serving Size 172 g

Amount Per Serving

Calories 244	Calories from Fat 43

	% Daily Value*
Total Fat 4.8g	7%
Saturated Fat 0.6g	3%
Trans Fat 0.0g	
Cholesterol 0mg	0%
Sodium 13mg	1%
Potassium 641mg	18%
Total Carbohydrates 39.7g	13%
Dietary Fiber 5.4g	22%
Sugars 6.7g	
Protein 10.7g	

Vitamin A 37%	•	Vitamin C 158%
Calcium 7%	•	Iron 22%

Nutrition Grade A

* Based on a 2000 calorie diet

Zucchini pasta salad

Serves: 1

Time: 15 minutes

Ingredients:

- 1 tablespoon Greek yogurt
- 1 tablespoon extra-virgin olive oil
- ¼ avocado, diced
- ¼ cup cherry tomatoes
- ¼ cup spinach
- ¾ cup spiraled zucchini
- ¼ cup edamame, shelled
- ¼ cup celery, chopped
- ¼ cup yellow bell pepper, chopped
- 2 tablespoons feta cheese
- Salt and pepper – to taste

Directions:

1. Place the yogurt, olive oil, avocado, spinach, salt and pepper in standard Mason jar; apply the blender base and transfer the jar onto blender; process until you have smooth dressing.
2. Top the dressing with ingredients in following order; celery, yellow bell pepper, edamame, tomatoes and zucchini pasta.
3. Apply the jar lid and shake well before use.

Nutrition Facts

Serving Size 249 g

Amount Per Serving

Calories 387 | Calories from Fat 291

	% Daily Value*
Total Fat 32.4g	**50%**
Saturated Fat 7.4g	**37%**
Trans Fat 0.0g	
Cholesterol 17mg	**6%**
Sodium 251mg	**10%**
Potassium 915mg	**26%**
Total Carbohydrates 16.3g	**5%**
Dietary Fiber 7.7g	**31%**
Sugars 3.5g	
Protein 12.9g	

Vitamin A 44%	•	Vitamin C 103%
Calcium 25%	•	Iron 18%

Nutrition Grade B+

* Based on a 2000 calorie diet

Mediterranean couscous salad

Serves: 1

Time: 10 minutes

Ingredients:

- 1 garlic clove, minced
- 1 tablespoon olive oil
- ½ tablespoon shallots, minced
- ½ lemon, juiced and zested
- ½ cup couscous, cooked
- ½ cup can garbanzo beans, drained and rinsed
- ¼ cup can cannellini beans, drained and rinsed
- ¼ cup can black beans, rinsed and drained
- ¼ cup feta, crumbled
- ¼ cup cucumber, seeded and diced
- ¼ cup tomato, diced
- Salt and pepper – to taste

Directions:

1. Place the garlic, olive oil, shallots, lemon juice and zest, salt and pepper in standard Mason jar; apply the jar lid and shake the ingredients until combined.
2. Top the dressing with; cucumber, garbanzo beans, tomatoes, cannellini beans, black beans, couscous and feta cheese.
3. Chill before serving.

Nutrition Facts

Serving Size 316 g

Amount Per Serving

Calories 649	Calories from Fat 206

	% Daily Value*
Total Fat 22.9g	35%
Saturated Fat 7.7g	39%
Trans Fat 0.0g	
Cholesterol 33mg	11%
Sodium 761mg	32%
Potassium 580mg	17%
Total Carbohydrates 89.0g	30%
Dietary Fiber 9.1g	36%
Sugars 3.7g	
Protein 22.5g	

Vitamin A 12%	•	Vitamin C 14%	
Calcium 26%	•	Iron 18%	

Nutrition Grade B-

* Based on a 2000 calorie diet

Barley salad

Serves: 2

Time: 30 minutes

Ingredients:

- ¼ cup barley, uncooked
- 2 tablespoons extra-virgin olive oil
- 1 tablespoon fresh parsley, chopped
- 3oz. feta cheese, diced
- ¼ cup olives, pitted and chopped
- ¾ cups cherry tomatoes, quartered
- 6 spears asparagus
- Salt and pepper – to taste

Directions:

1. Cook barley in medium pot of boiling water; reduce heat and simmer for 20 minutes or until barley is cooked.

2. Rinse barley under cold water and drain well; place aside.
3. Cook the asparagus with very small amount of oil cook asparagus, over medium heat, until tender. Chop coarsely.
4. Layer the ingredients, starting with barley and followed by asparagus, tomatoes, feta, olives and parsley, all dividing between two wide mouth Mason jars. Drizzle with olive oil and season to taste before serving.

Nutrition Facts

Serving Size 239 g

Amount Per Serving

Calories 360	Calories from Fat 231

	% Daily Value*
Total Fat 25.6g	39%
Saturated Fat 8.8g	44%
Cholesterol 38mg	13%
Sodium 630mg	26%
Potassium 448mg	13%
Total Carbohydrates 25.2g	8%
Dietary Fiber 6.9g	28%
Sugars 5.1g	
Protein 11.3g	

Vitamin A 30%	•	Vitamin C 27%
Calcium 26%	•	Iron 19%

Nutrition Grade B+

* Based on a 2000 calorie diet

Guacamole salad

Serves: 1

Time: 10 minutes

Ingredients:

- 3 tablespoons extra-virgin olive oil
- 2 tablespoons lime juice
- 1 tablespoon cilantro, chopped
- ¼ teaspoon hot sauce
- 3 tablespoons red onion, chopped
- 1 teaspoon jalapeno, seeded and diced
- 1 tomato, medium, diced
- 3 cups mixed salad greens
- 1 tablespoon cilantro, fresh and chopped
- ½ avocado, peeled and cubed
- Salt and pepper

Directions:

1. Add olive oil, lime juice, cilantro, hot sauce, salt and pepper in a standard Mason jar. Apply the jar lid and shake well.
2. Add the onion, followed by the jalapeno and diced tomato. Layer on the mixed salad greens and cilantro.
3. Top all with cubed avocado and sprinkle with squeeze of lime juice.
4. Chill slightly before serving.

Nutrition Facts

Serving Size 659 g

Amount Per Serving

Calories 656	Calories from Fat 559

	% Daily Value*
Total Fat 62.1g	95%
Saturated Fat 10.2g	51%
Trans Fat 0.0g	
Cholesterol 0mg	0%
Sodium 151mg	6%
Potassium 1410mg	40%
Total Carbohydrates 27.5g	9%
Dietary Fiber 8.2g	33%
Sugars 3.5g	
Protein 8.1g	

Vitamin A 111%	•	Vitamin C 199%
Calcium 8%	•	Iron 20%

Nutrition Grade B

* Based on a 2000 calorie diet

Tangy quinoa salad

Serves: 1

Time: 10 minutes

Ingredients:

- 2 tablespoons Greek yogurt
- Juice from ¼ lime
- 1 tablespoon extra-virgin olive oil
- 1 tablespoon cilantro, chopped
- ¼ teaspoon minced garlic
- 1 pinch cumin
- ½ tablespoon rice vinegar
- ½ cup cooked quinoa
- ¼ cup can black beans, rinsed and drained
- ¼ cup can corn
- 1 cup spinach
- ¼ cup sliced tomatoes
- ¼ avocado, diced

- Salt – to taste

Directions:

1. Place the yogurt, lime juice, olive oil, and cilantro, garlic, cumin and rice vinegar in a Mason jar; apply the lid and shake well until blended.
2. Top the dressing with spinach, tomatoes, quinoa, black beans, corn and avocado.
3. Stir well or shake before use.

Nutrition Facts

Serving Size 340 g

Amount Per Serving

Calories 651	Calories from Fat 269

	% Daily Value*
Total Fat 29.9g	46%
Saturated Fat 4.8g	24%
Trans Fat 0.0g	
Cholesterol 0mg	0%
Sodium 397mg	17%
Potassium 1304mg	37%
Total Carbohydrates 81.3g	27%
Dietary Fiber 14.4g	57%
Sugars 3.3g	
Protein 18.9g	

Vitamin A 67%	•	Vitamin C 34%
Calcium 12%	•	Iron 39%

Nutrition Grade B+

* Based on a 2000 calorie diet

7 layers salad

Serves: 1

Time: 10 minutes

Ingredients:

- 2 tablespoons extra-virgin olive oil
- Juice and zest of 1 lemon
- ¼ cup can black beans
- ¼ cup can cannellini beans
- ¼ cup green beans, blanched
- 2 tablespoons corn
- ¼ cup cucumber, seeded and diced
- 2 tablespoons red onion, diced
- 1 tablespoon yellow bell pepper, chopped
- 1 tablespoon fresh parsley, chopped
- Salt and pepper – to taste

Direction:

1. Place the lemon juice, zest, olive oil and pinch of salt and pepper in a standard Mason jar; apply the blender base onto jar process the ingredients until smooth.
2. Place the onions in the jar, followed by black beans, bell pepper, corn, green beans, cannellini beans and parsley.
3. Apply the lid and shake well before serving.

Nutrition Facts

Serving Size 281 g

Amount Per Serving

Calories 411	Calories from Fat 261

% Daily Value*

Total Fat 29.0g	45%
Saturated Fat 4.1g	21%
Trans Fat 0.0g	
Cholesterol 0mg	0%
Sodium 254mg	11%
Potassium 760mg	22%
Total Carbohydrates 36.6g	12%
Dietary Fiber 10.4g	42%
Sugars 3.4g	
Protein 11.1g	

Vitamin A 17%	Vitamin C 42%
Calcium 9%	Iron 25%

Nutrition Grade B-

* Based on a 2000 calorie diet

Pear-spinach-pomegranate salad

Serves: 1

Time: 10 minutes

Ingredients:

- ½ cup pomegranate seeds
- 3 tablespoons sherry vinaigrette
- 2oz. blue cheese, crumbled
- 3 cups spinach leaves, divided
- 1 pear, cored, peeled and sliced
- ¼ cup pecan nuts, chopped

Directions:

1. Add vinaigrette at the bottom of a Mason jar; place over sliced pear.
2. Place 2 cups of spinach on top of the pears, add pomegranate seeds, ½ cups spinach and chopped pecans. Finish with remaining spinach.
3. Shake well before use.

Nutrition Facts

Serving Size 336 g

Amount Per Serving

Calories 337   Calories from Fat 152

	% Daily Value*
Total Fat 16.8g	26%
Saturated Fat 10.7g	53%
Trans Fat 0.0g	
Cholesterol 43mg	14%
Sodium 864mg	36%
Potassium 809mg	23%
Total Carbohydrates 34.3g	11%
Dietary Fiber 6.6g	27%
Sugars 18.5g	
Protein 15.6g	

Vitamin A 178%	•	Vitamin C 57%
Calcium 40%	•	Iron 17%

Nutrition Grade B+

* Based on a 2000 calorie diet

Quinoa-mushrooms salad

Serves: 1

Time: 10 minutes

Ingredients:

- ½ tablespoon balsamic vinegar
- ½ small shallot, chopped
- ½ tablespoon honey
- 1 ½ tablespoons extra-virgin olive oil
- ¼ garlic clove, minced
- 1 small carrot, grated
- 1oz. mushrooms, sliced
- 1oz. green olives, sliced
- ¼ cup quinoa, cooked
- 5 cherry tomatoes, halved
- 1 cup baby spinach

Directions:

1. Combine vinegar, shallot, honey, olive oil and garlic in a standard Mason jar. Apply the lid and shake well.
2. Top dressing with; carrot, mushrooms, olives, quinoa, tomatoes and baby spinach.
3. Apply the lid and shake before serving.

Nutrition Facts

Serving Size 220 g

Amount Per Serving	
Calories 428	Calories from Fat 232

	% Daily Value*
Total Fat 25.7g	40%
Saturated Fat 3.6g	18%
Trans Fat 0.0g	
Cholesterol 0mg	0%
Sodium 318mg	13%
Potassium 673mg	19%
Total Carbohydrates 44.8g	15%
Dietary Fiber 5.9g	24%
Sugars 11.7g	
Protein 8.5g	

Vitamin A 225%	•	Vitamin C 22%
Calcium 10%	•	Iron 26%

Nutrition Grade B

* Based on a 2000 calorie diet

Tuscan bean salad

Serves: 1

Time: 10 minutes

Ingredients:

- 2 tablespoons Tuscan dressing, store-bought
- 1 tablespoon Kalamata olives
- ¼ cup diced tomatoes
- ¼ cup diced cucumbers
- ½ cup cannellini beans
- 1oz. Romano cheese
- 1 cup baby spinach

Directions:

1. Place the dressing in a jar; top with cucumbers, tomatoes, beans, olives, Romano cheese and baby spinach.
2. Apply the jar lid and shale well.
3. Serve after.

Nutrition Facts

Serving Size 230 g

Amount Per Serving

Calories 445   Calories from Fat 86

% Daily Value*

Total Fat 9.5g	15%
Saturated Fat 5.1g	26%
Trans Fat 0.0g	
Cholesterol 29mg	10%
Sodium 462mg	19%
Potassium 1631mg	47%
Total Carbohydrates 60.6g	20%
Dietary Fiber 24.5g	98%
Sugars 4.0g	
Protein 32.2g	

Vitamin A 67%	•	Vitamin C 33%
Calcium 48%	•	Iron 50%

Nutrition Grade A

* Based on a 2000 calorie diet

Waldorf salad in jar

Serves: 1

Time: 10 minutes + inactive time

Ingredients:

- ½ cup spiralized apples
- ¼ lemon
- 1 cup spiralized cucumber
- ¼ cup chopped celery
- 1 cup Boston lettuce
- 1 tablespoon walnuts, crushed
- ¼ cup Greek yogurt
- ½ tablespoon extra-virgin olive oil
- ½ tablespoon apple cider vinegar
- Salt and pepper – to taste
- 2-3 drops cinnamon liquid stevia

Directions:

1. Squeeze lemon over apples and place aside in a bowl.
2. Place yogurt, olive oil, cider vinegar, pinch of salt and pepper and liquid stevia in a standard Mason jar; apply the lid and shake well.
3. Add celery in the jar followed by apples, cucumber and lettuce; top with walnuts.
4. Cover and refrigerate for 20 minutes.
5. Shake well before serving.

Nutrition Facts

Serving Size 207 g

Amount Per Serving

Calories 137	Calories from Fat 107

% Daily Value*

Total Fat 11.8g	18%
Saturated Fat 1.3g	7%
Trans Fat 0.0g	
Cholesterol 0mg	0%
Sodium 26mg	1%
Potassium 342mg	10%
Total Carbohydrates 7.0g	2%
Dietary Fiber 1.8g	7%
Sugars 2.7g	
Protein 3.0g	

Vitamin A 5%	•	Vitamin C 11%	
Calcium 3%	•	Iron 12%	

Nutrition Grade B

* Based on a 2000 calorie diet

Paleo salad with mustard vinaigrette

Serves: 1

Time: 10 minutes

Ingredients:

- 1 tablespoon extra-virgin olive oil
- ¼ tablespoon mustard, Dijon style
- 1 teaspoon lemon juice
- ½ teaspoon balsamic vinegar
- Salt and pepper – to taste
- 1 cup Romaine lettuce
- 2 tablespoon carrot, shredded
- 2 tablespoons red bell pepper, chopped
- 2 tablespoons cucumber, chopped
- ½ tablespoon sunflower seeds
- ½ tablespoon fresh parsley, chopped

Directions:

1. Place the olive oil, mustard, lemon juice, vinegar, salt and pepper in a standard Mason jar; apply the jar lid and shake until blended.
2. Add the bell pepper, cucumber and carrots, followed by sunflower seeds, parsley and lettuce.
3. Shake before use.

Nutrition Facts

Serving Size 129 g

Amount Per Serving

Calories 165	Calories from Fat 142

	% Daily Value*
Total Fat 15.8g	24%
Saturated Fat 2.1g	11%
Trans Fat 0.0g	
Cholesterol 0mg	0%
Sodium 16mg	1%
Potassium 227mg	6%
Total Carbohydrates 6.1g	2%
Dietary Fiber 1.8g	7%
Sugars 2.6g	
Protein 1.7g	

Vitamin A 61%	•	Vitamin C 54%
Calcium 3%	•	Iron 12%

Nutrition Grade B-

* Based on a 2000 calorie diet

Ratatouille salad

Serves: 1

Time: 50 minutes

Ingredients:

- ½ eggplant, small, cut into medium pieces
- 1 garlic clove, minced
- Salt and pepper – to taste
- ½ tablespoon extra-virgin olive oil
- ½ cup chickpeas, cooked
- 1 tablespoon onion, chopped
- 1 new potato, small, peeled and diced
- ½ tablespoon balsamic vinegar
- 3oz. can whole tomatoes
- 1 zucchini, spiralized
- Pinch of dried oregano
- 1 tablespoon very thin tahini

Directions:

1. In a small sauce pot combine eggplant, potatoes, onion, garlic and spices. Add 2 tablespoons water and cook until vegetables are soft, for 15-20 minutes, stirring. Stir in the tomatoes, breaking up with wooden spoon. Remove from the heat.
2. Add remaining ingredients, except noodles and tahini, and bring to gentle boil; reduce heat and simmer for 25 minutes.
3. Place the zucchinis in a Mason jar; top with prepared ratatouille and drizzle with thin tahini before serving.

Nutrition Facts

Serving Size 638 g

Amount Per Serving

Calories 541	Calories from Fat 125

% Daily Value*

Total Fat 13.8g	21%
Saturated Fat 1.7g	9%
Trans Fat 0.0g	
Cholesterol 0mg	0%
Sodium 180mg	7%
Potassium 1948mg	56%
Total Carbohydrates 86.5g	29%
Dietary Fiber 28.8g	115%
Sugars 23.7g	
Protein 25.0g	

Vitamin A 20%	•	Vitamin C 84%
Calcium 20%	•	Iron 45%

Nutrition Grade A

* Based on a 2000 calorie diet

Blueberry, spinach and blue cheese salad

Serves: 1

Time: 10 minutes

Ingredients:

- 3 cups baby spinach, divided
- 2oz. crumbled blue cheese
- ¼ cup sliced almonds
- ½ cup blueberries, fresh
- 2 tablespoons red wine vinegar
- 3 tablespoons extra-virgin olive oil
- ½ tablespoon minced shallot
- Salt and pepper –to taste

Directions:

1. Place the vinegar, olive oil, shallots, salt and pepper in a bowl; whisk until blended.
2. Place 3 tablespoons of the vinaigrette blueberries in a standard Mason jar; add blueberries and top with 2 cups spinach, followed by almonds.
3. Top with remaining spinach and finally blue cheese.
4. Shake well before use.

Nutrition Facts

Serving Size 323 g

Amount Per Serving

Calories 770	Calories from Fat 637

% Daily Value*

Total Fat 70.8g	109%
Saturated Fat 17.6g	88%
Trans Fat 0.0g	
Cholesterol 43mg	14%
Sodium 865mg	36%
Potassium 916mg	26%
Total Carbohydrates 21.3g	7%
Dietary Fiber 6.7g	27%
Sugars 9.0g	
Protein 20.4g	

Vitamin A 179%	•	Vitamin C 62%
Calcium 46%	•	Iron 26%

Nutrition Grade B-

* Based on a 2000 calorie diet

Ranch chicken salad

Serves: 1

Time: 10 minutes

Ingredients:

- ¼ cup mayonnaise
- ½ lemon, juiced
- 1 teaspoon chives, fresh, minced
- ¼ cup sour cream
- 3oz. chicken, cooked and cut into pieces
- 3oz. cooked pasta
- ½ red bell pepper, chopped
- 1 tablespoon fresh parsley, minced
- ¼ teaspoon dried dill
- ¼ teaspoon garlic powder
- ¼ teaspoon onion powder
- 1 cup lettuce
- Salt and pepper – to taste

Directions:

1. Combine sour cream, mayonnaise, garlic powder, onion powder, lemon juice, parsley, chives, salt and pepper in a standard Mason jar; add in pasta and stir until combined.
2. Top with chicken, bell pepper and lettuce; serve after.

Nutrition Facts

Serving Size 407 g

Amount Per Serving

Calories 758   Calories from Fat 329

                                  % Daily Value*

Total Fat 36.6g	56%
Saturated Fat 11.4g	57%
Cholesterol 168mg	56%
Sodium 532mg	22%
Potassium 648mg	19%
Total Carbohydrates 69.7g	23%
Dietary Fiber 1.9g	8%
Sugars 7.3g	
Protein 37.8g	

Vitamin A 56%	•	Vitamin C 142%
Calcium 12%	•	Iron 33%

Nutrition Grade B-

* Based on a 2000 calorie diet

Egg salad

Serves: 1

Time: 10 minutes

Ingredients:

- 2 hardboiled eggs
- ¼ cup mayonnaise
- ½ cup arugula
- 2 pickles, diced
- Salt and pepper – to taste

Directions:

1. Dice the hardboiled eggs and place in a bowl; season to taste and add mayonnaise; stir until combined.
2. Transfer the mixture into wide mouth jar and pickles; top with arugula and chill before serving.

Nutrition Facts

Serving Size 287 g

Amount Per Serving

Calories 372	Calories from Fat 258

	% Daily Value*
Total Fat 28.7g	44%
Saturated Fat 5.7g	28%
Cholesterol 343mg	114%
Sodium 2114mg	88%
Potassium 190mg	5%
Total Carbohydrates 18.0g	6%
Dietary Fiber 1.7g	7%
Sugars 6.0g	
Protein 12.3g	

Vitamin A 21%	•	Vitamin C 5%
Calcium 7%	•	Iron 13%

Nutrition Grade C+

* Based on a 2000 calorie diet

Turkey-chickpea salad with pa vinaigrette

Serves: 2

Time: 10 minutes

Ingredients:

- 1 cup turkey meat, cooked and shredded
- ½ apple, diced and tossed with some lemon juice – to prevent browning
- 2 tablespoons celery, diced
- ¼ cup cucumber, seeded and diced
- ¼ cup tomatoes, chopped
- ½ cup cooked chickpeas
- 2 tablespoons dried cherries
- 2 tablespoons chives, chopped
- 2 tablespoons water
- Juice of ½ lemon
- ½ cup fresh peas
- 2 mint leaves, chopped
- Salt and pepper

Directions:

1. Place the peas, water, mint, lemon juice, salt and pepper in food blender; process until smooth and divide evenly between two standard Mason jars.
2. Top the pea dressing with shredded turkey, chickpeas, cucumber, celery, dry cherries, apples, tomatoes and chives, dividing all between the jars.
3. Shake well or stir before serving.

Nutrition Facts

Serving Size 263 g

Amount Per Serving

Calories 362	Calories from Fat 62

% Daily Value*

Total Fat 6.8g	11%
Saturated Fat 1.5g	8%
Trans Fat 0.0g	
Cholesterol 53mg	18%
Sodium 71mg	3%
Potassium 884mg	25%
Total Carbohydrates 43.6g	15%
Dietary Fiber 12.2g	49%
Sugars 13.1g	
Protein 32.7g	

Vitamin A 14%	•	Vitamin C 42%
Calcium 7%	•	Iron 61%

Nutrition Grade A

* Based on a 2000 calorie diet

Asian cabbage salad with peanut dressing

Serves: 2

Time: 15 minutes

Ingredients:

- 1 cup Napa cabbage, chopped
- 1 cup red cabbage, chopped
- ½ cup red bell pepper, chopped
- ½ cup carrots, thinly sliced
- ½ cup edamame, shelled and cooked
- ¼ cup peanuts
- ½ cup cilantro, chopped
- 1/3 cup vegetable oil
- 2 tablespoons rice wine vinegar
- ½ tablespoon honey
- ¼ cup radishes
- ½ teaspoon soy sauce
- ½ tablespoon peanut butter
- ½ teaspoon minced ginger, fresh
- Juice from ¼ lime

Directions:

1. Place the oil, vinegar, honey, soy sauce, peanut butter, ginger and lime juice in food blender; process until blended thoroughly.
2. Divide the dressing between two standard Mason jars; begin layering salad; place the red cabbage, then radishes, Napa cabbage, bell pepper, carrots, edamame, and top with peanuts. Apply the lids on the jars and shake well before serving.

Nutrition Facts

Serving Size 283 g

Amount Per Serving

Calories 605   Calories from Fat 467

% Daily Value*

Total Fat 51.9g	80%
Saturated Fat 9.3g	47%
Trans Fat 0.0g	
Cholesterol 0mg	0%
Sodium 163mg	7%
Potassium 902mg	26%
Total Carbohydrates 23.1g	8%
Dietary Fiber 7.3g	29%
Sugars 9.6g	
Protein 15.8g	

Vitamin A 146% •	Vitamin C 136%
Calcium 21% •	Iron 24%

Nutrition Grade B-

* Based on a 2000 calorie diet

Spring salad with flowers

Serves: 1

Time: 10 minutes

Ingredients:

- 2 tablespoons extra-virgin olive oil
- 1 tablespoon balsamic vinegar
- ½ teaspoon dried basil
- ½ teaspoon onion powder
- 1 teaspoon dried parsley
- ¼ cup cucumber, seeded and chopped
- ¼ cup tomato, diced
- ¼ cup arugula
- ¼ cup spinach
- 2 tablespoons raw pistachio
- 1 tablespoon apricots, dried and chopped
- Some edible flowers

Directions:

1. Add olive oil, vinegar, basil, onion powder and dried parsley in a standard Mason jar; apply the lid and shake until combined.
2. Top the dressing with cucumber, tomatoes, arugula, spinach, pistachios, apricots and edible flowers. Apply the lid once again and shake until ingredients are coated with the dressing.
3. Serve immediately.

Nutrition Facts

Serving Size 157 g

Amount Per Serving

Calories 357   Calories from Fat 318

	% Daily Value*
Total Fat 35.4g	54%
Saturated Fat 4.9g	24%
Trans Fat 0.0g	
Cholesterol 0mg	0%
Sodium 12mg	1%
Potassium 425mg	12%
Total Carbohydrates 9.9g	3%
Dietary Fiber 2.9g	12%
Sugars 4.3g	
Protein 4.5g	

Vitamin A 33%	•	Vitamin C 22%	
Calcium 5%	•	Iron 7%	

Nutrition Grade B-

* Based on a 2000 calorie diet

Tabbouleh salad

Serves: 1

Time: 10 minutes + inactive time

Ingredients:

- ¼ cup bulgur
- 1 cucumber, chopped
- 2 tomatoes, chopped
- 1 spring onion, sliced
- ¼ cup mint, fresh, chopped
- ¼ cup fresh parsley, chopped
- 2 tablespoons extra-virgin olive oil
- 1 tablespoon lemon juice
- Salt and pepper – to taste

Directions:

1. Soak the bulgur in cold water for 30 minutes; drain and place in a sieve for 20 minutes to get rid of excessive liquid.
2. Combine oil, lemon juice, salt and pepper in a standard Mason jar; apply the lid and shake well; add bulgur.
3. Top the bulgur with cucumber, tomatoes, spring onion, parsley and mint.
4. Apply the lid once more and shake well before use.

Nutrition Facts

Serving Size 680 g

Amount Per Serving

Calories 473	Calories from Fat 268
	% Daily Value*
Total Fat 29.7g	46%
Saturated Fat 4.4g	22%
Trans Fat 0.0g	
Cholesterol 0mg	0%
Sodium 45mg	2%
Potassium 1417mg	40%
Total Carbohydrates 51.3g	17%
Dietary Fiber 13.4g	53%
Sugars 12.4g	
Protein 10.0g	

Vitamin A 94%	•	Vitamin C 125%
Calcium 16%	•	Iron 35%

Nutrition Grade A

* Based on a 2000 calorie diet

Chef salad

Serves: 1

Time: 10 minutes

Ingredients:

- 1 cup Iceberg salad, chopped
- ½ cup shredded carrots
- ¼ cup cucumber, sliced
- 4 mushrooms sliced
- 4 grape tomatoes, halved
- 1 hardboiled egg, sliced
- ¼ cup shredded cheddar cheese
- 2 tablespoons diced ham
- 2 tablespoons red onion, chopped
- ¼ cup cashews, soaked in water
- 2 tablespoons olive oil
- 1 tablespoon lemon juice
- 1 teaspoon garlic powder
- Salt and pepper – to taste
- ½ teaspoon basil, dried

Directions:

1. Toss the cashews, olive oil, lemon juice, garlic powder, basil, salt and pepper in a standard Mason jar.
2. Apply the blender base on the jar and blend the ingredients until smooth.
3. Top the dressing with mushrooms, tomatoes, cucumbers, red onion, carrots, ham, cheese, lettuce and egg.
4. Apply the lid and shake well before use.

Nutrition Facts

Serving Size 351 g

Amount Per Serving

Calories 705	Calories from Fat 535

	% Daily Value*
Total Fat 59.5g	91%
Saturated Fat 15.1g	75%
Trans Fat 0.0g	
Cholesterol 203mg	68%
Sodium 510mg	21%
Potassium 867mg	25%
Total Carbohydrates 25.7g	9%
Dietary Fiber 4.2g	17%
Sugars 8.5g	
Protein 24.4g	

Vitamin A 205%	•	Vitamin C 28%
Calcium 28%	•	Iron 31%

Nutrition Grade A-

* Based on a 2000 calorie diet

Fruit Based Salads

Cold fruit salad

Serves: 1

Time: 10 minutes + inactive time

Ingredients:

- ¼ cup pineapple chunks, fresh
- 4 strawberries, hulled and sliced
- ¼ cup blueberries
- ¼ cup watermelon, diced
- 2 tablespoon raspberries
- A dollop of whipped cream

Directions:

1. Place the pineapple chunks in the bottom of standard Mason jar.
2. Top with strawberries, blueberries, watermelon and raspberries.
3. Cover and refrigerate for 20 minutes.
4. Top with a dollop of whipped cream.

Nutrition Facts

Serving Size 179 g

Amount Per Serving

Calories 76	Calories from Fat 4

	% Daily Value*
Total Fat 0.5g	1%
Trans Fat 0.0g	
Cholesterol 0mg	0%
Sodium 2mg	0%
Potassium 212mg	6%
Total Carbohydrates 19.0g	6%
Dietary Fiber 3.6g	14%
Sugars 13.0g	
Protein 1.2g	

Vitamin A 5%	•	Vitamin C 101%
Calcium 2%	•	Iron 6%

Nutrition Grade A

* Based on a 2000 calorie diet

Fruit trifle salad

Serves: 2

Time: 10 minutes

Ingredients:

- ¼ cup pineapple chunks, fresh
- 4 strawberries, hulled and sliced
- ¼ cup seedless green grapes
- 1 banana, sliced
- ¾ cup milk
- ¼ cup sour cream
- 4oz. crushed pineapple
- 1.5oz. instant banana pudding

Directions:

1. Place pineapple in the bottom of Mason jar.
2. Top with strawberries, grapes and banana slices; cover and place in the fridge.
3. Whisk the milk and sour cream in a bowl; add pudding and mix until blended. Finally stir in pineapple chunks and spread over chilled fruit salad. Serve after.

Nutrition Facts

Serving Size 377 g

Amount Per Serving

Calories 299	Calories from Fat 86

	% Daily Value*
Total Fat 9.5g	15%
Saturated Fat 5.7g	28%
Trans Fat 0.0g	
Cholesterol 25mg	8%
Sodium 283mg	12%
Potassium 556mg	16%
Total Carbohydrates 49.8g	17%
Dietary Fiber 3.2g	13%
Sugars 23.4g	
Protein 7.2g	

Vitamin A 9%	•	Vitamin C 99%
Calcium 24%	•	Iron 3%

Nutrition Grade B

* Based on a 2000 calorie diet

Fruit salad with tangerine sauce

Serves: 1

Time: 12 minutes

Ingredients:

- 1 tangerine, finely chopped
- 4 strawberries, hulled
- ¼ cup pineapple chunks, fresh
- ¼ cup raspberries, fresh
- ¼ green apple, diced
- ¼ cup tangerine juice
- 1 tablespoon sugar
- ¼ tablespoon butter

Directions:

1. Prepare the sauce; heat the sugar and butter in small sauce pan and heat over medium heat until sugar starts to dissolve. Turn on the heat and cook, stirring, until mixture starts to caramelize.
2. Pour in tangerine juice and chopped tangerine; bring mixture to gentle bubble and cook for 2 minutes more; pace aside to cool.
3. Pour the sauce into standard Mason jar; top with pineapple, strawberries, raspberries and apples; apply the lid and shake well before use.

Nutrition Facts

Serving Size 243 g

Amount Per Serving

Calories 169   Calories from Fat 30

	% Daily Value*
Total Fat 3.4g	5%
Saturated Fat 1.8g	9%
Trans Fat 0.0g	
Cholesterol 8mg	3%
Sodium 25mg	1%
Potassium 297mg	8%
Total Carbohydrates 37.0g	12%
Dietary Fiber 5.1g	20%
Sugars 30.0g	
Protein 1.4g	

Vitamin A 13%	•	Vitamin C 135%
Calcium 3%	•	Iron 5%

Nutrition Grade B+

* Based on a 2000 calorie diet

Fruit salad with avocado

Serves: 1

Time: 10 minutes

Ingredients:

- ½ pink grapefruit, segmented
- ¼ cup blackberries, fresh
- ½ avocado, cubed
- 2 teaspoons honey
- 2 tablespoons walnuts, crushed
- 2 tablespoons thick yogurt

Directions:

1. Combine the yogurt and honey in a Mason jar.
2. Top with avocado, grapefruit, blackberries and walnuts.
3. Stir well before serving.

Nutrition Facts

Serving Size 243 g

Amount Per Serving

Calories 389	Calories from Fat 261
	% Daily Value*
Total Fat 29.0g	45%
Saturated Fat 4.7g	23%
Trans Fat 0.0g	
Cholesterol 0mg	0%
Sodium 7mg	0%
Potassium 750mg	21%
Total Carbohydrates 33.2g	11%
Dietary Fiber 12.7g	51%
Sugars 18.9g	
Protein 6.7g	

Vitamin A 12%	•	Vitamin C 85%
Calcium 4%	•	Iron 8%

Nutrition Grade B

* Based on a 2000 calorie diet

Fruit salad with mint-lime dressing

Serves: 1

Time: 10 minutes + inactive time

Ingredients:

- ¼ cup strawberries hulled and quartered
- 1 kiwi, peeled and sliced
- ¼ cup pineapple chunks, fresh
- ¼ cup raspberries, fresh
- 2 tablespoons water
- 2 tablespoons sugar
- 2 tablespoons fresh mint leaves, chopped
- Zest of ¼ lime

Directions:

1. Bring water and sugar in small sauce pan to boil; stir until sugar is dissolved.
2. Remove from the heat and stir in the mint and lime zest.
3. Let it steep for 15 minutes and strain in standard Mason jar.
4. Top the dressing with pineapple, strawberries, kiwi and raspberries.
5. Stir gently or shake before serving.

Nutrition Facts

Serving Size 248 g

Amount Per Serving

Calories 189	Calories from Fat 8

% Daily Value*

Total Fat 0.8g	1%
Trans Fat 0.0g	
Cholesterol 0mg	0%
Sodium 8mg	0%
Potassium 435mg	12%
Total Carbohydrates 47.8g	16%
Dietary Fiber 6.3g	25%
Sugars 37.9g	
Protein 2.1g	

Vitamin A 11%	•	Vitamin C 201%
Calcium 7%	•	Iron 12%

Nutrition Grade A

* Based on a 2000 calorie diet

Fruit salad with watermelon-mint dressing

Serves: 1

Time: 12 minutes

Ingredients:

- 1 plum, cubed
- 1 orange, segmented and cubed
- 1 pear, cubed
- ½ apple, cubed
- ½ cup watermelon chunks
- 4 strawberries, hulled and cubed
- 10 mint leaves

Directions:

1. Place the watermelon cubes in a standard Mason jar, followed by mint leaves.
2. Apply the blender base on the jar and blend the ingredients until smooth.
3. Top the fruit dressing with pear, apple, orange and strawberries; stir gently before serving.

Nutrition Facts

Serving Size 462 g

Amount Per Serving

Calories 230	Calories from Fat 6

% Daily Value*

Total Fat 0.7g	1%
Trans Fat 0.0g	
Cholesterol 0mg	0%
Sodium 3mg	0%
Potassium 665mg	19%
Total Carbohydrates 59.1g	20%
Dietary Fiber 11.9g	48%
Sugars 42.6g	
Protein 2.8g	

Vitamin A 9%	•	Vitamin C 232%
Calcium 9%	•	Iron 6%

Nutrition Grade A

* Based on a 2000 calorie diet

Limoncello fruit salad

Serves: 1

Time: 10 minutes

Ingredients:

- ¼ cup cantaloupe melon, diced small
- 1oz. strawberries, sliced
- ¼ cup blueberries
- ¼ cup pineapple chunks, fresh
- 1 tablespoon Limoncello liqueur
- ½ tablespoon fresh mint, minced

Directions:

1. Combine liqueur and mint in a standard Mason jar; top with pineapple, melon, strawberries and blueberries.
2. Apply the lid and shake gently to coat the fruits.
3. Serve after.

Nutrition Facts

Serving Size 134 g

Amount Per Serving

Calories 60	Calories from Fat 3

	% Daily Value*
Total Fat 0.3g	0%
Trans Fat 0.0g	
Cholesterol 0mg	0%
Sodium 6mg	0%
Potassium 129mg	4%
Total Carbohydrates 15.1g	5%
Dietary Fiber 2.5g	10%
Sugars 10.8g	
Protein 1.0g	

Vitamin A 5%	•	Vitamin C 88%	
Calcium 2%	•	Iron 6%	

Nutrition Grade A

* Based on a 2000 calorie diet

Tropical salad with spicy dressing

Serves: 1

Time: 10 minutes

Ingredients:

- 1 teaspoon fresh minced ginger
- ¼ teaspoon jalapeno, minced
- 1 tablespoon honey
- 2 teaspoons lime juice
- ½ teaspoon lime zest
- ½ cup star fruit
- ¼ cup oranges, sliced
- ¼ cup strawberries, sliced
- 1 kiwi, peeled and sliced

Directions:

1. Combine honey, lime juice, lime zest, jalapeno and ginger in a standard Mason jar.
2. Stir or shake well to combine; microwave foe 20 second on high; stir and microwave for 20 seconds more, or until bubbly.
3. Place aside to cool ad when cooled top with fruits, starting with star fruit, oranges, kiwi and strawberries.
4. Shake gently to coat the fruits before serving.

Nutrition Facts

Serving Size 235 g

Amount Per Serving

Calories 166	Calories from Fat 8
	% Daily Value*
Total Fat 0.8g	1%
Cholesterol 0mg	0%
Sodium 5mg	0%
Potassium 483mg	14%
Total Carbohydrates 41.6g	14%
Dietary Fiber 6.0g	24%
Sugars 32.3g	
Protein 2.3g	

Vitamin A 4%	•	Vitamin C 226%
Calcium 6%	•	Iron 4%

Nutrition Grade A

* Based on a 2000 calorie diet

Sparkling summer salad

Serves: 1

Time: 10 minutes

Ingredients:

- ¼ teaspoon orange zest
- ¼ teaspoon lemon zest
- 1 tablespoon orange juice
- 1 tablespoon lemon juice
- 2 tablespoons white grape juice
- ½ tablespoon honey
- 1 tablespoon sparkling wine
- ¼ cup seedless white grapes
- ¼ cup pineapple chunks, fresh
- ¼ cup honeydew melon, diced
- 2 tablespoons strawberries, sliced
- 2 tablespoons blueberries

Directions:

1. Place orange zest, orange juice, lemon zest, lemon juice, honey and white grape juice in small sauce pan.
2. Bring to boil and reduce heat to low; simmer for 5 minutes. Place aside to cool and when cool pour into Mason jar; stir in the sparkling wine.
3. Top the dressing with pineapple, honeydew melon, white grapes, strawberries and blueberries.
4. Shake gently and serve.

Nutrition Facts

Serving Size 219 g

Amount Per Serving

Calories 107   Calories from Fat 4

	% Daily Value*
Total Fat 0.4g	1%
Trans Fat 0.0g	
Cholesterol 0mg	0%
Sodium 12mg	1%
Potassium 291mg	8%
Total Carbohydrates 26.9g	9%
Dietary Fiber 1.9g	8%
Sugars 23.3g	
Protein 1.1g	

Vitamin A 1%	•	Vitamin C 123%
Calcium 2%	•	Iron 5%

Nutrition Grade A

* Based on a 2000 calorie diet

Poppy seeds fruit salad

Serves: 1

Time: 10 minutes

Ingredients:

- ¼ cup strawberries, hulled and quartered
- ½ teaspoon poppy seeds
- ½ tablespoon orange juice
- 1 tablespoon honey
- 2 tablespoons sour cream
- ¼ teaspoon lemon zest, grated finely
- ¼ cup banana, sliced
- ¼ cup kiwi, sliced
- ¼ cup apples, diced
- ½ orange, segmented and sliced

Directions:

1. Combine honey, poppy seeds, sour cream and orange juice in a standard Mason jar.
2. Top with apples, orange, banana slices, kiwi and strawberries.
3. Gently shake before serving.

Nutrition Facts

Serving Size 292 g

Amount Per Serving

Calories 256	Calories from Fat 57

	% Daily Value*
Total Fat 6.3g	10%
Saturated Fat 3.3g	16%
Trans Fat 0.0g	
Cholesterol 11mg	4%
Sodium 16mg	1%
Potassium 595mg	17%
Total Carbohydrates 52.0g	17%
Dietary Fiber 6.1g	25%
Sugars 39.9g	
Protein 3.2g	

Vitamin A 9%	•	Vitamin C 206%
Calcium 11%	•	Iron 5%

Nutrition Grade B+

* Based on a 2000 calorie diet

Mixed fruit salad with citrus dressing

Serves: 1

Time: 10 minutes

Ingredients:

- ¼ cup strawberries, hulled ad sliced
- ¼ cup pineapple, fresh
- 1 mandarin orange, sliced
- 2 kiwis, sliced
- ¼ cup mango chunks
- ¼ teaspoon poppy seeds
- 2 tablespoons honey
- ¼ teaspoon mandarin orange zest
- ¼ teaspoon grated ginger
- 1 tablespoon lemon juice
- ½ tablespoon lime juice

Directions:

1. Add lime juice, lemon juice, ginger, zest, honey and poppy seeds in a standard Mason jar; apply the jar lid and shake well.
2. Top the dressing with the pineapple, mango, mandarin orange, kiwi and strawberries.
3. Shake gently and serve.

Nutrition Facts

Serving Size 334 g

Amount Per Serving

Calories 295   Calories from Fat 13

	% Daily Value*
Total Fat 1.4g	2%
Trans Fat 0.0g	
Cholesterol 0mg	0%
Sodium 10mg	0%
Potassium 626mg	18%
Total Carbohydrates 73.9g	25%
Dietary Fiber 7.1g	29%
Sugars 61.4g	
Protein 2.9g	

Vitamin A 10%	•	Vitamin C 335%
Calcium 8%	•	Iron 6%

Nutrition Grade A

* Based on a 2000 calorie diet

Mojito fruit salad

Serves: 1

Time: 10 minutes

Ingredients:

- ¾ cup watermelon, diced
- ¼ cup strawberries
- 1oz. raspberries
- 1oz. blueberries
- 1 tablespoon packed mint
- 1 ½ tablespoons lime juice
- 1 teaspoon powdered sugar

Directions:

1. Place lime juice, powdered sugar and packed mint in a standard Mason jar; apply the lid and shake well.
2. Add watermelon, strawberries, raspberries and blueberries; shake gently and serve.

Nutrition Facts

Serving Size 209 g

Amount Per Serving

Calories 86	Calories from Fat 5
	% Daily Value*
Total Fat 0.5g	1%
Cholesterol 0mg	0%
Sodium 2mg	0%
Potassium 247mg	7%
Total Carbohydrates 21.3g	7%
Dietary Fiber 3.7g	15%
Sugars 15.3g	
Protein 1.5g	

Vitamin A 13%	•	Vitamin C 71%
Calcium 2%	•	Iron 6%

Nutrition Grade A

* Based on a 2000 calorie diet

Made in the USA
Middletown, DE
18 March 2017